Light
Caught
Bending

Martha Modena Vertreace

diehard
Edinburgh

diehard
publishers
3 Spittal Street
Edinburgh
EH3 9DY

ISBN 0 946230 28 5
Copyright Martha Modena Vertreace 1995

British Library Cataloguing in Publication Data
A catalog record for this book is
available from the British Library

The publisher acknowleges the financial assistance of the Scottish Arts Council in the publication of this volume.

By the same author

Second House from the Corner, pub Kennedy-King College
Under a Cat's Eye Moon, pub Clockwatch Review Press

Other **diehard** poetry

The Rhondda Sonnets, Tony Rees
The Divine Joker, Richard Livermore
Millennial, Sally Evans

Poetry–related **diehard** drama

Klytemnestra's Bairns, Bill Dunlop
Gang Doun wi a Sang, a play about William Soutar,
by Joy Hendry
Alcestis, by George Buchanan

A full list of current **diehards** is available on request

for my parents;

Walter Charles Vertreace
Modena Kendrick Vertreace

All roads lead to death, but some roads lead to things which can never be finished. Wonderful things.
– Ben Okri: The Famished Road

the Author
and the book.

Born Washington D.C., 1945, grad. M.A. Roosevelt University, Chicago, currently Assistant Professor of English at Kennedy-King College, Chicago, Martha M. Vertreace's poetry has won her a fair amount of recognition in Illinois and is fast becoming one of the names whispered on the international scene. Many of the pieces in *Light Caught Bending* have appeared in American magazines (unobtainable over here), and in Dublin. It is high time they were available in European book form.

We have reversed the age-old printers' convention that poems begin on an odd-numbered page and run over (which most poetry does these days) and begun them on the evens so that each opening gives a whole poem rather than the tail of the last and the head of the next, page 1 becoming a contents page to maintain conventional numbering. This isn't an Americanism **diehard** have picked up; it may catch on, it might not. But one thing is for certain; the world has not heard the last of Martha Modena Vertreace.

Contents

Evolution of Flight	2
Culture Shock	4
Earthworks	6
Light Caught Bending	8
Tiger Oak	10
Cyclogenesis	12
Weather Warnings	14
Dublin Aisling	16
Theatre of the Deaf	22
Village of the Mermaids	24
Summer Solstice	26
Lazarus of Blue Grass Lane	28
A Dream of Bright Green Leaves	30
Afterlife	32
A Document in Madness	34
Morning Star	36
Trans-Manche Link	38
Elmhurst-Chicago Stone Company	40
Pathfinder	42
Night Growth	44
In the Gloaming	46
The Work of Human Hands	48
Shapeshifters	54
London Snow	56
Eads Street	58
Ashes, Ashes	60

Evolution of Flight

Wrapped in shantung robes, a mandarin
    makes gravity
his loyal peasant, surveys his land
    as he hangs
from paper kites, black wings he shapes
    like cormorants
whose diving beaks turn shadows
    afloat on the river
into golden carp. Powered by rows
    of rockets, fireworks
sparking across morning sky, he
    tries to outdo
the monarch he envies – its wings mottled
    in fine embroidery,
its gentle easing into willing poppies.
    His own concubine
opens like hibiscus to his imperial sun
    out of fragrant habit.
Her lips pucker into crimped petals
    of painted carnations.

    From her father's sooty hut
where no oiled sheets cover the window
    in the room
where her family sleeps on stone, warmed
    by the hearth beneath it,
he leads her to her royal chamber,
    whose doors face
the courtyard. Drawn to small feet,
    bee-stung lips,

he ignores her tears, the thin hands
    of his dry wife
quivering in mimosa.

                  From separate windows,
the women watch clear sky, dreaming
    that double-happiness
inked in mulberry, laughing lines
    on rice paper,
cannot stop the dragon's tongue
    from burning flight feathers
one by one, from dropping his godself
    into the celestial maw.

Culture Shock

In the Reuters photo, Hong Kong, her body folded
more like a rag doll – abandoned
when a little girl grew bored with torn toys –
than woman, her leg swung over the edge,
her head dangled. Cotton shoes slipped
from the sixteenth floor while she hung wash

above her neighbour's apartment, awash
in baby things and underwear. She folded
like damp cloth on her neighbour's line, slipped
spread-eagle to the thirteenth, modesty abandoned
when clouds exploded, as gravity edged
her to fly with unwaxed toy

wings. More like her sons with toys
on the porch after nap time, faces washed
for dinner, the fire fighters edged
her from the clothesline, which folded
around her like a web abandoned
by the widow whose mate slipped

beyond her hungry grasp, slipped
during the Year of the Horse, as toy
lions danced in papier-mache abandon
to ward off demons. Her wash
floated piece by piece, folded
against the sidewalk. She knew the edge

too well, remembered how her mother's feet, edged
into golden lilies, would quietly slip
to her moonlit garden. Servants folded
silk mums on her path, she more favourite toy –
a rainbow carp – than wife. The past washed
over her, her mother's face abandoned

her to the cherry picker, as she abandoned
one century for the next. The edges
of her black silk pyjamas frayed, awash
in shame as strangers touched her, as she slipped
from one man to the next, an antique toy.
82 years old, in fair condition, she folded

under ancestral abandon, only to slip
to the edge as her body filled space, a toy
washed too clean, too neatly folded.

Earthworks

A dragonfly hovers over an invisible lake
of solid light, the windshield wherein he sees
his thousand eyes a thousand times reflected.
O'Connell Street sprawls under his wings
as cars crawl through rush hour.
The pane warms where the sun slants
mute behind a veil of scaffolding.

Near the Green, where purple spikes of foxglove
jab the air with their bending,
a crescent of aspens circles a fork lift.
Roots curl in burlap
like seeds unplanted, their packets sealed,
or bulbs unsprung.

> *Many of these women had been unwanted,*
> *shunned, or marginalised. Some were*
> *an embarrassment to their families.*

Luscious in her fountain of flowing hair,
Anna Livia waits to baptise infants,
holy water spilling down their heads
into the stone basin, then back
into Earth's womb.

Beyond the shared grave,
the simple iron cross, the power
of self-naming –
Still time. There is.
The seared scar of leaves turns toward the Equinox.

> *Society back in that time did not make
> space for such women. They came here
> from all over Ireland.*

Trapped where no one wanted women
with empty hands and nameless babes,
abandoned by parents whose shame
carved the scarlet **A** on daughters' breasts,
they headed for High Park Convent,
Drumcondra, in Dublin,
to hot water, lye soap,
vats of dirty sheets from Georgian houses.

In Latin, the word for *host* is the same
as for *guest* – who gives and who receives
a matter of the unboundaried heart.

> *We respected their confidentiality.
> We certainly never referred to anyone
> as a fallen woman.*

Years after the laundry closed –12 acres
sold in payment for debts –
113 women in consecrated ground,
the convent cemetery,
were exhumed, cremated, turned to ash,
reburied at Glasnevin
in a double plot washed clean
by the name they chose:
Magdalen.

Light Caught Bending

Straight rows and rows of frame homes
guard the sandy creek
where summer dreams are red grapes
on wet formica, the tap still dripping,
where heat rises in my mouth
with raw promises,
its power of invention unquestioned.

Near my mother's bedroom,
a flock of robins springs from honeysuckle,
from trefoil vines which bind the side fence
with tendrils, then starbursts,
compass points in twilight.

She waits for me to say
the road opens to you
bathed in blue light
go ahead without me
I'll hear your feet in tall grass
your shoulders part the fresh green
of plum leaves and I'll follow
as I let her hand slip from mine.

Her lips circling the *no* she gives me,
her black body sinks feet first
into black earth,
until knees, waist, breasts disappear
as ages whirl in a pool
of grey clouds, their flat bottom
a watermark on blank onionskin.

I know now why death is female;
her voice, a sultry alto
humming spirituals
folding stories into line-dried sheets.

Night lifts its velvet cowl over my head
against the chill. Sailors haul
their boats from the water,
free the harbour from its bondage
to desire; allow freezing sleep
which comes to make us think
all stops somehow –
the wave and particle, the shore.

Tiger Oak

Standing in twos, threes, hiding
   from low pressure,
gulls taste the smell of storm,
   crouch in the field
as a wake of blackbirds
   fans red epaulets
over sedge. Fog crawls west
   from the skittish lake
grown used to grinding ice
   along rubble-laid barriers.

   A short spring:
Slipping the rolled hem
   of a white handkerchief
up her dimity sleeve, she feels
   the same tingling her knees
become when rain soaks furrows,
   when corn grows strong,
redolent with June.
         She works
   to set right
the old house – full of furniture –
   before she leaves;
labels everything, knowing
   dreams once,
memories of dreams. Clouds drip
   to the roof
as she stretches to a yawn
   on her mother's sleighbed.
Tiger oak stripes an ancient cage
   around her.

A sparrow
lands on the sill, pecks at the glass,
   nestles under its wing –
good luck her grandmother once said,
   promised signs and wonders
more mundane.
         Ducks wade
in jagged teeth of early dandelions,
   tattered ghosts
blown across wind-bared roots
   of new-green ash.

She knows Earth cannot hold her,
dozes under a Strawberry Moon.

Cyclogenesis

{i}

Naked, lovely, warm, a woman
sleeps inside me,
listening to my grandmothers.
Head over my heart,
she counts beats,
stirs if one skips.
               Legs coil
at the base of my spine;
in the pit of my stomach,
her mound, dark as the new moon,
the no-moon I know
by ten thousand names, which waxes
when she prophesies over me
in a meadow of violet self-heal
circling a Norman tower
still erect at Howth Harbour
where dinghies tether.

{ii}
At twilight,
when worlds pass from hand to hand,
white buoys mark empty space;
seagulls dry on rows of wooden posts.
In a man's jacket
from a Dublin flea market – cuffs
lined in striped cotton
turned inside out,
as if the brooding tweed I love
mirrors flesh, bones;
as if a broken button, shoulder pads,
make sense of things – I tell her
I learned to ride at nine
a boy's bike; learned quick slip,
stumble, pain of the horizontal bar.

{iii}
Her smile crackles
electric like 1800 thunderstorms
trapped on Earth at any given time,
like time freeze-dried, sifting
through my body's veil.
In the morning
cushioned in grey sky,
the blood moon, sailor's warning,
is a counterfeit coin
with its face rubbed smooth,
not as solid as my curves,
not as baby-round,
when I find her gone.

Weather Warnings

Under a Chaste Moon so full of the coming storm
she thought she would drown
in deep breaths,
mist beading her upper lip, her cheeks, a woman
lets him lead, her palm on his arm. Wind
spills over them as they float

on currents of cool air, as if floating
means he keeps his hands in his pockets, a storm
withdrawn from the seaboard. He says the wind,
once roused, can lift her, drown
her in gusts too strong for womanly
ways. Gasping for breath,

she steadies herself, breathes
through her mouth, thinks of other hands floating
on waves of dark bronze – like a woman
soothes a child afraid of thunderstorms –
hands of Chinese students, Hong Kong, drowning
in plastic gloves. Ignoring the wind,

blind eyes admit no wind-
dried light; fingers see Rodin's *Thinker*, which breathes
for them alone. In the AP photo, smiles drown
in hopeless dark, then float
in a storm
of love for warm metal, a woman's

touch. The paper flies from her, a woman
who fears the wind-
strewn path spiralling into the storm's
eye. She holds her breath,
lets go his arm, floats,
waits to drown

as he had promised, drowning
in plain view, this woman,
floating
between street and wind,
tethered to a man breathing
storms.

This time, wind drowns his voice,
frees her womanly breath
as she floats beyond whatever storm he summons.

Dublin Aisling
{i}
Bewley's Oriental Cafe (Est. 1840)

Hooded crows preen on streetlamps
branched over Grafton Street,
tattered veil heavy with fog.
A fire eater – top hat and tails;
his companion tosses five red balls,
juggles them through tongues of flame
for the breakfast crowd.

Maeve fingers the corona
of her Patrick's cross
as if the sun were still Father of Heroes,
as torches spin like worlds afire.
Over her black smock, she bows
a white ruffled apron,
binds red ringlets of her wild hair
in black net, her grandmother's snood
under a pleated cap.

"The Great Tradition Lives On"
on every Comment Card.

She stands in the doorway
as first light finds under all black lace,
the certain round softness
a street artist celebrates
in jeans threadbare at the knees;
who stands a bowler on its crown, worn slick;
begs for silver pounds
where cobbles pinwheel buskers;
then chalks her as Snow White, her Seven Dwarfs
set dancing. Mist traps pastels
which cling until teatime rain
cleans stone canvas.

All night, a gale sucks water
from the Liffey's black pool,
drowns the attic floor.
Rust rings spread over pastries
laden with clotted cream, chocolate cherries,
as the manager catwalks the rafters –
then slips. His legs dangle through a foot-square hole
as plaster weakens above the jam pots
near the brass coffeemaker, eight roasts a day.
The queue winds around fruit scones,
rock buns, whiskey cake,
beyond the take-away counter
as the stream flows unchecked,
as heaven measures Earth in damp patches.

{ii}
In the Old World Balcony

On break, he dozes in red velvet comfort
of straight backed chairs,
dreams her walking up Otranto Place
around Scotsman's Bay
to the Tower; mounts a spiral stairwell
to the crown,
above the Forty Foot Bathing Place
forbidden to women
where she watches his broad back
as he leaps over brown smooth rocks
lying flat on the strand,
his strong waist and thighs
too beautiful to look at or ignore
then dives, jumps the breakers,
muscles taut under tight skin
as he swims naked –

dreams her gliding on green linoleum
between stacks of plates,
stained cups on walnut tables.
Bowing to some inner light,
she lifts trays, carries them behind the screen
as if all movement were of a piece – head,
hips, the swing of arms
one motion – unbound breasts,
small as robins' eggs, swaying.

Tomorrow Mæve will prove to him
that blue moons spy on emerald icebergs,
that ships float upside down in ocean
old as breath,
that light plays tricks with the mind
as if the past still flies
upright in liquid air
over Ben Bulben's grizzled face,
over grey cliffs chiselled
with his own creased face
until up no longer is,
nor down,
nor waves pound the sale foot
of Dun Ængus
where she will make him find
his own bread trail of crumbs.

He knows these are fairy tales she tells
to awaken little boys,
no longer afraid of the dark.

{iii}
Going Home to Half Moon Street

She leaves him beneath a row
of marble crosses,
visible from the lane,
where yews green too perfectly.
Each wrinkled trunk
anchors each upended cone,
a child's sticky-fingered confection
popped from the tray
with warm water,
more patience than she needs.
She had stood at the shaft of Newgrange
where the winter sun, newborn,
pierces three-sided spirals
whose meaning
only the stones know, secret
for Neolithic years.

Behind the wooden fence, the herd
waits with swollen udders
as wings unfurl a feather winding-sheet.
Whirling out of the round day-moon,
magpies pluck out cow eyes,
shiny bits of silver coins in a traveller's purse –
so the farmer says, eating
leftover rashers.

Across the street, a bay window glows
behind hard valerian climbing
the balcony of a Georgian gatehouse
glazed in bucketing rain.
A shade raises, lowers, raises again.

The farmer would drop her
at the station, his wife says,
auburn eyes counting Irish pounds she trades
for lodging – the double bed,
wooden chair, its seat too hard
for reading, unvacuumed floor –
and he does, after the pudding hour,
pushing the kitchen chair
against the wall.
Clinging to his shirt,
clumps of wool, red from the killing floor,
flecks of sawdust
scattered to keep him from sliding.

You are the man
who burns back rhododendrons to free the sun,
Mæve tells him, the same
who drives cows up the road,
the cream one balky under your shouting.

His mouth curves,
more accustomed to silence
than answering red-haired women.
For his bushy eyebrows, the wall
of his jaw, he could be
an artist's model, waiting for oil on canvas,
the smell of mad genius
which makes a peasant immortal.

In their own time, he whispers,
orange circles of lichen
level ancient mountains
to fields of fresh grass.

They drive through blind curves which stitch
the west to the east,
north to south.
The Wicklows grow luminous,
taller under grey clouds;
red bells of fuschia toll
from bush to bush of white elderflower.
Fog brings the smell of plaice,
salmon, cod from Dublin street stalls;
victuallers in Market Square open until the gloaming.

How many nights have you spent waiting,
she asks him, how many days
and nights?
The roadway to Dublin yields to the sign
"End of Hard Shoulders".

Theatre of the Deaf
– for Paul Keeley

With breathless speech, the actor follows
    line cues,
clipped consonants of Dublin English
    tongued under control
which the lead cannot hear, whose hand
    fill the room with words.

    His wide-eyed dreamstate:
madness fathers a red-haired doppelganger
    who sounds what is signed,
hapless guide to stage right –
    the mirrored clock
where ten-armed octopi slide
    into the breast pocket
of his waistcoat, where phrases bounce
    off padded cells.

    You trace the shape for *nightmare*
on your face – two fingers slide down closed eyes,
    cheeks, lips,
then toss in the bed your palm makes – a man,
    you say, straitjacketed
in shadow. You read more messages spelled
    in air,
want to live in the house those words lock
    shut before the drama ends.

On the Green, ducks sleep
behind a veil of branches, bills on their backs.
Woods fade, defy the dark,
as we leave Grafton Street, slipping
through stone walls,
wooden doors the guard opens
to my accent –
the password, the silver key I show him
while my hands tremble
from too much coffee, a night grown cold
under a new moon.

Village of the Mermaids
—after Paul Delvaux

They do not move, although it seems
they should, arms arced over their heads.
Instead their stiff-backed wooden chairs
face the street where lintels frame
closed doorways. House slats merge
toward the beach as the vanishing point
centres beyond mountains which lift
from the coast, from mansards.
Dresses tighten at the wrists. Hands
rest, one covers the other, collars rise
over full bosoms. Grosgrain hems
drag on shore to hide unwomanly scales.
Hair does not gentle foreheads,
nor does wind finger so careful
an arrangement which spills
between shoulders as waves. With eyes
too round, they gaze past each other,
past Delvaux who captures
this last moment before brine winds.
Knees press together as straight legs
curve in perfect fusion.
Already at the waterline, their sisters
yearn seaward with strokes the painter
cannot fathom – no feet for sand,
tails useful in currents. Their shadows
crosshatch the road where brittle shells,
a handful of pebbles break the flat bend.

It's done with mirrors, you tell me,
standing in the gallery. This, then,
is what we've come to – stars arow
like fishtail lights of the fifties' Cadillacs
my father could not afford.
Along the breakfront, the stone mermaid
waits for winter, for crystal skin
which hides her until spring moulting.

The sun in clear sky, the moon
in October, rain softens into evening.
In the beginning, the garden
we never left. Lightning strikes Earth
one hundred times every second
as I take your arm,
pull you close to me.

Summer Solstice

Estimated number of time capsules buried worldwide: 10,000
— *Harper's Index*

> At sixteen, my mother's sheath
> against darkness or unquiet space
>
> after my father dies, I share her bed.
> she wonders what scares me most as a child.
>
> Carrs Beach – rain chases Sunday School classes
>   from salty waves dockside
> to Capitol Transit buses which Beulah Baptist
>   hires for the annual picnic.
> With the Busy Bees, straw basket on his lap,
>   my father
> in flowered walking shorts my mother made
>   sits beside me, aisle-side
> so I can watch rain spatter Chesapeake Bay.
>   Parked where log posts
> reach the bottom frame of the windshield
>   another bus houses
> Pansies, girls with high breasts whose braids
>   mirror ours
> but longer.

                    In menthol fog, my mother,
            their chaperone,
stands straight as a clothespin doll,
            close-cropped auburn yarn
for hair.
                    Their driver backshifts as dun light
            grains gritty windows
tricks me into believing her face calm,
            pencilled eyebrows
still, her bus unmoving while ours glides
            toward the edge
of the jetty.
                    At six, I haunt chlorine pools
            enough to know
the sound of drowning.
                    Should I walk with her
            on hot sand
or swim with him where brine wraps us
            in sea-green foam?

The one question time cannot answer.
We sleep like silver spoons,

my head on her back as I count each breath,
as sudden death nestles in her very bones.

Lazarus of Blue Grass Lane

Germantown, Tennessee – *Swept along by rushing rainwater, a six-year-old Germantown boy survived a harrowing underground ride in the city's drainage system Friday.*

{i}
what was it like? – the reporter asks, years
after Jeffrey grabbed the bar,
climbed the ladder, squeezed into daylight

mud-stinking like a still-born calf
through curbside street grating.
Marshall Field's, where northshore ladies

curve pinkies with gemstone rings
over the black-tiled coffee bar: steam
whirls through the cappuccino brewer.

She hunches over Viennese cinnamon,
pesters for a slant to her story.
No visible injuries according to the doctor,

yet she read stormwater sucked him
into a Forgey Park culvert, wrapped him

shivering in the birth sac

of his yellow shirt, slushed him
three-quarters of a mile through canals
built for flood run-off.

{ii}   He uncrosses
then crosses his legs, his left ankle
rests squarely on his knee.
          So what
happened? – she wonders, nudges
the cassette recorder near his demitasse.
He stirs espresso silt without looking up,
shrugs his shoulders.
          She skims
old quotes in the Tribune: "I was
very scared" and "I got up on my feet
and I fell down" and "I was thinking
this was a dream."
          Nothing more
to tell.
{iii}
     His sleep remembers two blue moons,
December's astral hands which snatch him
from Lori's eleven-year-old grasp,

plunge him in the concrete ditch.
Liquid fingers glide between his legs,
his sex shrivels inside him.
          Blackness
first, then cold speed slaps his face
as it floats above the muck which pushes

toward the gutter at Blue Grass Lane,
toward his father who calls him forth –
     "I turned the corner and when I saw

     the yellow shirt I knew he was safe" –
his strong hands ready to break
the surface, pull him headfirst

slippery and screaming
     into the living afternoon
          night after night after night.

A Dream of Bright Green Leaves

When the Moon is seen beside an upside-down tree,
the tree is perceived as just a shape, not a tree
— *New York Times*

The colour of February stains slate roofs
whose sad open faces mirror morning.
Over Campbell Hills, skeins of crows tangle,

fling shadows against thick windows
which mimic weight-bearing walls
of the half-empty cafe where we sit

watching the Moon, too large
on the horizon, loom among bare elms,
the Great Miami sluggish with new ice.

A child fighting sleep, I do not give
my tears willingly to you
who smother my breathless hands in yours.

Scared of dawn, I step through blue snow;
cracked floes shift your words like silver nets.

A red ball rises.
                Frost on stubble grass
is red. Red, too, grey rocks in crystal houses;
maples in their red absence of buds,

red memory of Spring. Time to go,
you say.
      I think of Robert Goddard
who ate apples, my mother said,
like a horse; popped a russet whole

in his mouth then smiled to show
crisp peel on his tongue which turned
the fruit, crushed against his teeth

until it pulped
then spit out stem and seeds.

Afterlife

If a seed opens, swollen in water, can its white flower
bloom? A grave's food chamber six feet under opens
to free adzuki beans, rice, hundreds of Japanese seed
which flow over the scientist's hands like water
trays he stirs for three months until one seed swells,
which he pots. It grows an eight-petal magnolia, white

like clouds which gown snow-tipped Fujisan in white
robes of mourning. But why a seven-foot flower?
Because the ancients know that more than grain swells
the human heart, its green need for open
space as we face the sun, or water,
useless beauty we need to make sure our seed

prepares for what is foretold – that seeds
of death sprout at birth to fog the whites
of our eyes. Blood still recalls that water
first cradles us; we blossom like flowers
budding inside caves which we alone open.
Now birches peel off dry prophecies, as bark swells

in darkened runes we barely read, through cities swell
with our progeny, aware that bedded seeds
make good their promise, open
in rich black soil or white
sand. What stuns belief are flowers
which sleep two thousand years, as water

pools in a chemical dream. Earthbound, our water-
logged bodies beg stars for answers when the swell
of dirt and ice in the comet's head flowers
as it flies too close to Jupiter. Gravity seeds
the heavens with glittering white
shards, as if black holes open

for us; instead, a Theban tomb opens.
A mummy wears silk in her hair, though no hot water
softens cocoons for the Silk Road. No white
mulberry leaves feed the worm which swells
among the branches, no offering of seeds
buys more time. Precisely the point: flowers

bloom whether seeds open, like us,
from dust and ashes, or whether the white swell
of water bids them flower forth.

A Document in Madness

and mermaid-like awhile they bore her up...
— *Hamlet*

Monarchs dry wings on the undersides of leaves
    as rain flues cobblestone streets,
copper spires. Tile roofs glaze the cracked grin
    of a man who knows nothing of joy,
high breasts of the woman who turns to him.
    On folded arms, Ophelia sleeps
at her dinette.
    A jelly jar holds potpourri;
    rosemary and pansies; fennel and
columbines; rue and violets. Her gown matches
    curtains, tablecloth, darkly floral.
Blue ache of moonlight stumbles in willows,
    spills down her apron.
Her face is blue, her hands.
    She dreams
of Langelinie Harbour
flat stones where the Little Mermaid sits,
    whose nightmares vandals
haunt – pour red paint over her tail, cut off
    her head, weld it again –
as she forgives the Baltic Sea whose neap tide
    cannot save her.
    Light plays
tricks, sails triangles along cabinets,
    counters, as shutters filter
rays through bay windows. Her father's ghost
    floats unseen from room
to room. Spirits cannot cross rivers; mermaids
    brown as wave-smoothed amber,
forbidden to touch land.

Ophelia follows
when plate-glass faults
eddy like fingerwhorls whose bevelled rim
cuts feet which stand too close,
framed within the oak sash. Garlands of nettles,
crowflowers, daisies, long purples,
bind her wrists. Where ground slopes, she walks
upside-down. Catalpas sink
white blossoms with billowing skirts, watery roots
lift above the solid mast of trunk.

Morning Star

In cosmic space, fire-red, a probe flies
to the heart of myth: Venus in red
silk clouds, as the Magellan probes
our daydreams, in space
one Venus-year. With no moon, her cosmic
dance inspires such fire.

What do you know of fire,
earth no longer young as Venus-time flies
twice as fast? Magellan rips cosmic
veils one by one. She, high on CO_2, red-
faced, feigns shame as outer space
draws no drape past eyes which probe

Devana Chasma rift valley, then probe
the core where lava flows, source of fire
where crust splinters, spaces
fill with magma. The robot craft flies
over wilderness plains. Fault lines redden
as we dream of volcanoes which spew cosmic

tales we tell each other, praying for cosmic
oceans to spawn scallops which we probe
to find a goddess, mermaid, lady in red –
someone to enkindle earthly fire.
Radar decodes our maps, to fly
modules when embers die as space

widens between us. Pilots seek time-space
theories in books with blank pates, cosmic
notions of once-upon-a-time which fly
like moths around blind eyes. Probe
deep. Deny my ring of fire
draws you, jealous of the red-

tailed hawk that orbits your house, as red
moonset hazes your field glasses. Your space
fuses into his spiral which centres the fire
of his dive on yielding prey. His cosmic
will – to claim Earth as we probe
sky for stories through which we fly –

to probe fire-red cosmic space, to fly again.

Trans-Manche Link

Not China two hundred feet in slough
    ten miles off the coast, but a nautilus
        whose aquatic jets, ninety tentacles

propelled it through Cretaceous muck
    ninety-five million years ago
        between what became England and what

became France. Plumbing a side access duct
    hand-dug for air, the surveyor stumbled
        on the find: sixty pounds, twelve inches wide,

whose squid-like spawn rode Pacific currents.
    Rail tunnels yielded nothing, scooped by drills
        which bored a patch through what remained

    of fossil bone or flesh. Human hands pushed
    age aside more gently. Soft skin wrapping

his skeleton, far fewer arms, the man measured
    what linked this rock shell which supplied
        quite a briny mouthful of slate-grey meat

to a seafaring cave-dweller,
    the ivy chain which sagged its green weight
        across the parlour casement window,

    and a vacation story he retold
    at the reception. The channel project

complete, he swizzled his clear drink
    in a plastic glass. Ice cubes shifted
        like buoys in strong water. "I swam too far

from the windward side of Colima," he said
    "when a wave drove me to sea, my wife onshore
        like bleached driftwood. Surge kneaded,

rolled me like maize dough in bakers' hands
    at the taqueria. The undertow showed
        treasure hoards no one found – shipwrecks,

grottoes, piles of empty shells – then
    two friends joined me, floated for an hour
        until the boat moored, and I wondered

        whether there were more pressed stones,
        past lives to crack open,
        more stars in the universe than grains
        of sand on the white beach
        where my wife stood soaked in sunlight,
        and I knew there were."

Elmhust-Chicago Stone Company

{i}
Blackbirds rise like ghosts above dirt strips
which edge the quarry, then twist
to the highway. No river bevelled these planes

nor wind sheared smooth;
no ice-dark glacier scooped
these slopes. Car windows frame

the pit like rectangular beads,
a rosary flowing too fast to pray. Kneeling
on the back seat, her son waves

at diggers whose yellow hard hats bounce
sun in his eyes as he counts
dump trucks, cranes.

"Is it the end of the world,
Mama?" he asks as a crosswind swirls
dust over the rock face.

{ii}
A lampshade globe from the five-and-dime
waits on its tilted axis, a primed
whirling top – continents, islands, oceans,

mountains inked in bas-relief,
blues, purples, faded greens
adrift in honeyed cream. "Use a low-

watt bulb," the sales clerk said as he packed
the sphere in brown sacking,
"to make it glow."

Too dry to trust the electric day,
Earth keeps quiet on her bookcase
near her keys. "This is your world," she told

    her son as he watched her spin
    the ball with her fingers,
    and him with nowhere else to go.

Pathfinder

Earth rotates on its axis faster in September than in March
— *Chicago Standard News*

> Past the mute brace of stone owls
> tethered wide-eyed to the nave roof
> of Saint Thomas, along the boulevard
> between blocks of night, streetlights
> spill gold onto clusters of oaks;
> bare branches sway as if caught
> in ecstasy, the dance of wind; limbs
> bend north toward the empty pier.
>
> Beyond the shoreline, nothing, as lake
> and sky dim in deepening grey. What
> sacred way is this where trees blaze
> like swords of angels?
>
> ❦
>
> When I reach
> your door, I want to say, "There,
> and there, Ralph, see how the mall
> still wears Italian lights icicles
> from moonswept tides." Instead
> I follow you to a round wooden table,
> two yellow chairs, a bayberry votive
> we do not burn
>
> ❦
>
> where I tell you
> how I lived all February
> with my father's dark-skinned ghost
> who read my journals, counted my poems,
> studied his features on my face
> when he thought I slept, warm
> in the pale arms of my room;

how one morning the year after he
died, my mother and I, unafraid
in the clear sun of her kitchen, watched
as a woodpecker chiselled in the elm
near the window; the scarlet down
of his head patch kindled into flame.

❦

My cupped hands open, but free no dreams
to give you before Earth speeds up
and whirls us to opposite poles
where stars hang upside-down. As I
rise to leave, you kiss both cheeks.

Outside, a rush of cries – talons, beaks,
a scatter of wings in a cold gust
as a storm rips cloudbanks. A gull
flies over us, feathers arched as they
yield to air currents, gliding on pain.
I think of O'Keeffe's crow skimming
snow-covered hills, casting no shadow
with vast black wings.

Night Growth

The snow stuns the sky into quiet
only the lake understands,
restive beyond the grey stone breakwater.

Across the street, my neighbour knows
a green hope weaves a wooden trellis
over a fresh-powdered walk, his jacket,

a plaid patch on the shed doorknob.
His brown daughter sprouts bud breasts
under her sweatshirt; twirls tendrils

of dark braids, then steadies the plank
with both hands as her eyes follow
his hammer's arc.

❦

In her, I am twelve
again, New Year's Eve: my mother and I
sleep early – she, in their pink room,

I where my brother and I share bunks,
walls not repainted pre-war blue
when we move in, little floor space

for second-hand chairs, desks,
chests-of-drawers. Weak springs
give as sheets twine her ankles.

Pillowing in premature wishes,
we fear silver bullets
in my neighbour's pistol, his bayou way

of killing earthbound ghosts
when the old year dies,
❦
and so it goes.
The last slats nailed in place,
the girl trails her father into a house
aflame with saffron light of melting snow,

holy surprise getting past the silence.
A nighthawk perches sideways in the ash
like a bundle of wet leaves, unfurls

her wings, then lifts into air
I thought too cold for flight.

In the Gloaming

Still too shy to hide inside each other,
    we think we take ourselves
too seriously, like blind desperation
    at eighteen,
yielding to bittersweet tyranny of hormones,
    the ex-prom queen
whose flabby arms beckon her husband,
    his healing touch
she knows by heart – until a building
    torches evening sky
and bricks redden with callous heat;
    firefighters with meathooks
nudge concrete chunks from charred timber.
    Grim faces tell
stories we would rather not hear
    during dinner,
ashes forming the face of God
    for the six o'clock news.
Then it hardly matters whether arson
    or accident swallows
linoleum floors. The staircase twists
    off the wall.
        With no basements
    in Key West,
fishermen whom hurricanes drown
    snag in flame trees,
palmetto, rubber. Crushed blossoms lure
    red-mouthed chameleons. Newts
taste the smell of death in pampas grass.

What counts
is the fall – visions of reaching hands
    that cannot reach far enough
through plumes of grit, blown roofs,
    the fall faster
than prayer.
        Sitting next to me, my hand
    on your knee, you speak
of turfcutters, layers of history pressed
    into the bog, winter fires
on harbour hills as sacred. Tea leaves
    spell your blessing
in your cup. My palm lines deepen
    as the living room steeps
in lavender scattered on the hearth.
    Tomorrow people will watch
for hints of our spent passion; for now,

    come closer. So little time
    remains in the gathering dark.

The Work of Human hands

{i}
(Midland Woman)

So much is accident, mere happenstance,
unnatural selection, the wrong exit
take on the cloverleaf, the faded map

trusted beyond the brief encounter of clarity,
when, tentative as a bed of ghostly ferns
etched on frosted living room windows,

the sky too suddenly blues,
drains of all mystery
when a six-ton mastodon stumbles on a log;

round feet sink into pond marl –
28 pothole footprints scoop a 75 yard trail
across what becomes Brennan's Michigan pasture,

the same Brennan who digs a pool
but finds a pile of bones, a mastodon butchered
for meat, too big, too clumsy to survive

> a tribe of stone clubs, frenzied hunger,
> a mad dash up the food chain.

In her campfire settlement, hunters
with long spearheads, grooved down the middle,
slew mammoths; then cured meat in pits

1200 years ago in what is now called
Texas, whose Clovis culture buried
no grave gift which secures her passage

beyond the blue hills, more faith
than I have watching a Jacob's ladder
of sparrows and red maple leaves

> lift and drop in wind rapt holiness,
> praising the moon's clear face.

What would she think of the AP photo, the woman
as handmaid whose ponytail flutters
under a babushka, who sweeps dust of Sepphoris

off 1500-year-old mosaics – hunting scenes
of bare-breasted women with spears,
a caped, curly-haired centaur

holding above his head
a bowl inscribed "the helping god,"
its offering of new wine

> the ripe seal of his godhead?

{ii}
(Along the Silk Road)

Where I live, railroad tracks link
the dry creekbed to the school
where girls dance an elephant dragon,
Chinese New Year. Hands link

the coattails of each child
in line, who bends over, trumpeting
until the playground is a twisting trunk

which snuffles the yard for food,
for treasure, for some hint
of what lasts.

These days, I blame
ragweed goldenrod pokeweed
whose berries colonists squeeze
to improve cheap wine,

every seed-bearing spore-bearing plant,
knowing that my father drinks
to ease his asthma

> 6000 years ago, a sculptor chips a banquet scene
> in bas-relief on the upper left panel of a seal
> for the Royal Cemetery: two people who sit
>
> at double-handled crock sip barley beer
> through long straws. At the Sumerian trading post
> of Godin Tepe, a common pictograph for beer –
>
> lines within a jar where pale yellow dregs
> collect; "I think a lot of serious drinking
> was going on here," the archæologist says
>
> who unearths storerooms full of barley
> amid shards with tell-tale stains of red wine.

Seeing white barns dot fields of sere corn,
goshawks atop telephone poles
like a string of grey words I leave unsaid,

I wonder which comes first after grain
is tamed – plain dark loaves of bread or beer?

{iii}
(Hopscotch)

Soon cranes hoist the last boat
from the harbour, wooden jetties no wider
than the broad shoulders of my father

as he walks over fresh water, steadies
his taut line which slides between silver waves;
web-footed gannets melt scratching of ice

which cling to pier pylons, leaving
the Potomac to itself,
        searching
    Chesapeake Bay for sweet-salt kisses
    where crabs scuttle across Seagull Beach;

jellyfish redden the backs of summer's children
who believe swells and white sand
all they need for Paradise.

        Under the bandstand,
boys frighten yellowjackets buzzing
around acrid mouths of swan-necked wine bottles

shaped like daughters who tire of blindfolds,
gin pints with the curved shoulders of wives
who join rather than fight. Empties stand

arow along the wetline where warm currents
break across glass lips while no wax
seals ears too eager to trust the siren's song.

        Nothing astonishes the blind eye
        as stories years unfold unevenly, as fog
        coats the orchard where deer nibble

the windfall of pine cones and broken branches,
acorns. Blown offcourse, a homing pigeon
rests in the eaves.

      On the kitchen table,
winter oranges float green in a plate
of sunlight, their hubs of white stars
ringed with pulp in pale cells

like time I try to save, or sidewalks
with cracks accepting the chalk
of childhood games – who wins or loses

a matter of the misplaced toe,
the flat stone thrown too far,
when no wave washes bottles to the shore

      with faded messages from my father –
      why he drinks, the secret he best keeps.

{iv}
(E pur, si muove)

From his rooftop observatory, Siena,
Galileo learns the secret
of Jupiter's four harvestmoons

with his handmade astronomical telescope,
the galaxy suddenly grown larger
and more wild; he frees Earth,

lifting from her back
the burden of cosmological perfection,
as Heaven spins out of orbit, escapes

the hands of priests who hold the key,
chanting "God fixed Earth
upon its foundation, not to be moved
forever."

    He explodes
the abstract, mechanical categories
of preachers who assure me

that the Road to Hell is paved
with snifters melted in New World furnaces,
fenced in concrete rimmed with broken bottles
to fend off the poor.

    Kneeling
to save his body, Galileo says
"abjured, cursed, detested,"

of heresy too great to speak,
that Earth's hidden Eden circles
a mere created thing, more fire devil

than source of light or heat;
rising to save his soul, he murmurs,
"but even so, it does move" –

beyond the rim of judgment,
the if-then summation of human weakness.

Leaded with blue veins, my mother's
trembling hands are stained glass

I see through, clear to the other side
of the sanctuary.

Shapeshifters

Past midnight, the channel selector
corners a twenties' movie queen

who whirls barefoot in black and white,
silk gown at her ankles.

A lace collar frills off her breasts
as mist crosses the forest of grey oaks,

a river of fog awakens in the wrong bed.
Strings of lightning fray to the ground

where screams hang in her throat like seaweed
in willows after hurricanes

named for male saints.
          A snow ghost,
her image doubles on my troubled screen,

the four palms of her hands
cupped as if catching fireflies for lanterns –

mayonnaise jars with punctured lids –
stars trapped in glass

          like the young girl,
mildly retarded, whose heart's interest

in locker rooms full of naked boys
outstrips her mind's ability to understand,

who cannot refuse, cannot risk angering
them, who stare, tingly and moist,

like heroes do in movies, she would say.

At the end of the reel, the Wolf Moon
spawns the hairy monster we come to expect,

all fangs and claws, silent as well,
before the screen goes dead.

London Snow

Spring thaw in December: Mille Lacs fissures
into arks on which the chosen float to salvation.
New York Times:
>*Twenty-five people were rescued
Sunday after the ice they were fishing on
broke free and drifted more than half a mile
into a lake in east-central Minnesota.*

Floes yield
to trembling current, shudder, wake of time
which Galileo measured in pulsebeats
as he sought heaven in the baptistery,
Cathedral of Pisa.

The shadow
of the altar lamp paced marble halls
like a woman walking from door to window
watching for the postman who brings
airmail letters from overseas. Parchment
crackles like new fire which scours
my hearth wall:
>*One person looked down
at the fishing hole and notice rocks
going by and could not understand why
water was moving so rapidly.*

         I fold
the paper, pages sag to the rug
when the telephone gathers your Old World voice
in static fog. You plan a Sunday drive
to Lake District when north roads clear. Cars
stall on M6 motorway near Coventry
as Midlands frost.
         I speak of amber darkness,
mulling my words in your rosewood bowl.
Drink, I tell you.
         When you ring off,
the Gulf Stream brushes the sun which rose
too soon in liquid sky, brindled with messages
from ancient galaxies.
         What pendulum
sweeps past Greenwich Meridian then back
to my time zone?
         Lakefront rime shapes
your face in terrazzo, each perfect piece
set in grey stone, in slate clouds
which flow through bare branches
of nameless trees, as dreams freeze
in London snow.

Eads Street

{i}

Nothing comes of storm clouds stacked along the horizon
 like loaves of stale bread
on dusty Midwest shelves. For thirty days the pattern
 sets: lawns brown like carnations
drooping from flat chests of prom queens. Trace rain
 retreats from stressed roots
of stunted corn, as tassels shower pollen which no silk
 carries to flowers' heart.
Along the Ohio, barges run aground by day, held fast
 by shallows; by night, no traffic stirs.

Drought lowers the Sebring water table under central
 Florida topsoil. Limestone caverns
collapse, water draining, then dissolving clay and rock.
 The ground opens, a sinkhole swallows
one house. A resident notes: "The roof's almost even
 with the road around it." A second
lingers at the edge. The geologist: "We rarely if ever
 get any that far south."

{ii}

Year of the Dragon between May's two full moons:
    my mother's house evaporates.
The sofa leaves first, its plastic slipcovers shred
    like maple leaves covering our porch
during early Autumn; fled to the neighbours, leading lamps,
    end tables, beds out the back door.
Snapshots silt the front doorsill – me, stiff braids
    and no teeth; brother and father
like mismatched twins; her, the cautious flirt
    of hand-tinted portraits.

Knives, forks fly out the window, then sherbet glasses
    Blue Willow china, crocheted table linen.
The house creaks and groans, looking for her among five
    empty chambers, her footsteps
far too light to bend floorboards. My brother and I
    hold hands, wander room to room,
but cannot find her who twirls in blue light, in gossamer,
    prima ballerina where silk peonies
fray in a black cloisonne vase, we who long for rain,
    its know-nothing fall.

Ashes, Ashes

Palm fronds – lashing
the bare patch of ground
where lightning strikes,
dividing night between black
and burn,
and strikes, so nothing

grows, nothing –
mean hurricane – a lashing
surge, the white-hot burn
of surf against the ground
against tile roofs of pastel houses, black
with fear, struck

mute with fear. Yachts strike
the pier, rope tethers snap. Nothing
works, unbuilt as shutters rip. Blackened
wires lash
electric ground
as waves thrash and burn

where sea salt burns
Florida's coast. The full moon strikes
the wind-blind eye, slowly spinning, grounded
by a wall of rain. Nothing
else – no offshoot twister – lashes
flame trees whose black

roots strangle black
sky. Sunrise burns
homegrown tent cities, lashes
Sicily miles east as Etna strikes
village orchards, vineyards. Nothing
plugs lava searing the ground

where a green branch grounds
holy cards in ash. Blackened,
martyred saints stop nothing;
nor does a table set, candles burning,
wine and bread to strike
a bargain. Instead, a pear tree lashes

into bloom. Farmers lash the lacquered ground
as morning strikes against black clouds
a cleansing burn. Nothing lived for dies.